First World War
and Army of Occupation
War Diary
France, Belgium and Germany

57 DIVISION
170 Infantry Brigade
King's Own (Royal Lancaster Regiment)
2/5th Battalion
1 April 1919 - 30 April 1919

WO95/2979/8

Published by

The Naval & Military Press Ltd

Unit 10 Ridgewood Industrial Park,

Uckfield, East Sussex,

TN22 5QE England

Tel: +44 (0) 1825 749494

www.naval-military-press.com

www.nmarchive.com

This diary has been reprinted in facsimile from the original. Any imperfections are inevitably reproduced and the quality may fall short of modern type and cartographic standards.

© **Crown Copyright**
Images reproduced by permission of The National Archives, London, England, 2015.

Contents

Document type	Place/Title	Date From	Date To
Heading	WO95/2979-8		
Heading	2/5th Bn. K.O.R. Lancs Jan To May 1919		
War Diary	Agnez-Les-Duisans (Lens 11 3 H 97)	00/01/1919	00/01/1919
War Diary	Agnez Les Duisans (Lens 1:100,000 3 H)	00/02/1919	00/02/1919
Heading	2/5th Battalion The King's Own (Royal Lancaster) Regiment War Diary Month Ending 31st March 1919		
War Diary	Agnez-Les-Duisans (Lens 1:100,000 3 H)	00/03/1919	00/03/1919
War Diary	Agnez-Les-Duisans France Map Ref Lens II 1/100,000 3 R.65.65	01/04/1919	30/04/1919
War Diary	Agnez Les Duisans	00/05/1919	00/05/1919

worst case (8) 2n-1 2n-1 (8)

2/5th Bn K.O.R.Lancs
Jan to May 1919.

170 Bde

Index

SUBJECT.

WAR DIARY

No.	Contents.	Date.
	5 DIVISION	
	G.S.	
	February 1915	

WAR DIARY
or
INTELLIGENCE SUMMARY

2/5 Bn. The King's Own (R. Lanc.) Reg.

Vol 25 Feb 1919

Place	Date	Hour	Summary of Events and Information	Remarks and references to Appendices
AGNEZ LES DUISANS (LENS 1:100,000 8H)	Feb		During this month the battalion has remained at AGNEZ-LES-DUISANS engaged on salvage & training. Demobilization has continued and about 240 NCOs & men have left for dispersal. Detached duties have absorbed the majority of the men. Still on the strength of the unit. The Concert party has broken up after a very successful run.	

Lt Col P McNicoll
Commanding
2/5 Bn. THE KING'S OWN R. LANCASTER REGT

2/5th Battalion The King's Own (Royal Lancaster) Regiment.

War Diary

Month ending 31st March, 1919.

Army Form C. 2118.

2/5th Bn. The King's Own
(R. Lanc.) Regt.

WAR DIARY
or
INTELLIGENCE SUMMARY.
(Erase heading not required.)

Instructions regarding War Diaries and Intelligence Summaries are contained in F. S. Regs., Part II. and the Staff Manual respectively. Title pages will be prepared in manuscript.

Place	Date	Hour	Summary of Events and Information	Remarks and references to Appendices
AGNEZ-LES-DUISANS (REFS 1:100,000 3. H)	March 1919		The Battalion is now down to cadre strength, having demobilized all the other releasable men. Drafts of retainable men & volunteers for the Army of Occupation have been sent to the 1/5th Bn. The King's Own	

C. A. Hutchinson Capt
2/5 Bn K.O.R.L.R.

WAR DIARY
or
INTELLIGENCE SUMMARY.

(Erase heading not required.)

2/6 R Lenn Army Form C. 2118.

Place	Date	Hour	Summary of Events and Information	Remarks and references to Appendices
AGNEZ-LES DUISANS FRANCE MAP REF. LENS II. 1/100,000 3.R.65.b.5.	1st April 1919 30 April 1919		The Battalion has been down to cadre strength the whole of the month and ready to proceed to England. All the men have been regimentally-employed, and it has not been possible to have parades.	

J M G Mount Lt. Colonel,
Commanding
2/6th Bn. The King's Own (R.L.) Regt.

War Diary
2/5 Bn The King's Own (R Lanc Reg)

May 1919

AGNEZ LES DUISANS	The Battalion Cadre has remained at AISNE CAMP during this month, awaiting orders to proceed home. Early in the month the numbers were reduced from 46 O.R.s to 36 O.R.s. During the last week a further reduction to 12 O.R.s was notified, but orders to prepare to move to England ruled have left the normal strength unaltered. (Orders to entrain en route for England on the 2" June have been received)

C H Hudleston
Capt A/A/y
2/5 KORL

2/5 KORL

www.ingramcontent.com/pod-product-compliance
Lightning Source LLC
Chambersburg PA
CBHW081513160426
43193CB00014B/2681